THE ADVENTURES OF
LINCOLN AND LAMBY

BY ROBYN MATOS

Copyright © 2022 ROBYN MATOS
All Rights Reserved. Printed in the U.S.A.

Published by Two Penny Publishing
850 E Lime Street #266 Tarpon Springs, FL 34688
TwoPennyPublishing.com | info@twopennypublishing.com

No part of this publication may be reproduced, distributed, or transmitted in any form or by any means, including photocopying, recording, or other electronic or mechanical methods, without the prior written permission of the publisher, except in the case of brief quotations embodied in critical reviews and certain other noncommercial uses permitted by copyright law.

For permission requests and ordering information, email the publisher at:
info@twopennypublishing.com

ISBN: 978-1-950995-91-2
FIRST EDITION

For more information about the author or to book her for your next event or media interview, please contact her representative at: info@twopennypublishing.com

---

Two Penny Publishing is a partnership publisher of a variety of genres. We help first-time and seasoned authors share their stories, passion, knowledge, and experiences that help others grow and learn. Please visit our website: TwoPennyPublishing.com if you would like us to consider your manuscript or book idea for publishing.

This book is dedicated to my son Lincoln, who inspires me to use my imagination through his most trusted confidant,
Lamby.

Today was the day that was different from the others. It's the day all the kids WAVE GOODBYE to their fathers and mothers.

It was a day spoken of all summer long. To prepare them for when it was time to be S T R O N G.

The first day of school arrived, and Lincoln did NOT want to go. He cried and begged to stay home, but little did he know...

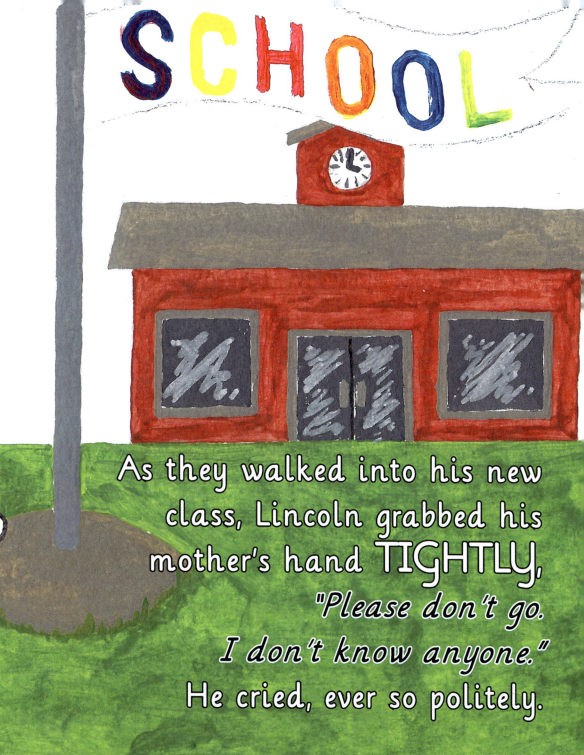

"Be brave. My boy,
I'll be back soon,"
Momma whispered in his ear,
"If you feel sad,
check your bag.
You'll see there's
nothing to fear".

Momma blew him a kiss
as she walked away, and
tears ran down his face.
Not a moment later,
he heard a little chatter
coming from someplace.

Lamby was very special to Lincoln,
she gave him the courage to be brave.
When she's around,
she also helps him listen and behave.
She gave him a quick wink and replied,

"Hey Linc!
Get ready for an awesome day!
I'm right here if you need me,
but I know you'll be okay!
Momma will be back later to
bring us both back home,
There's no need to be afraid,
for you are not alone."

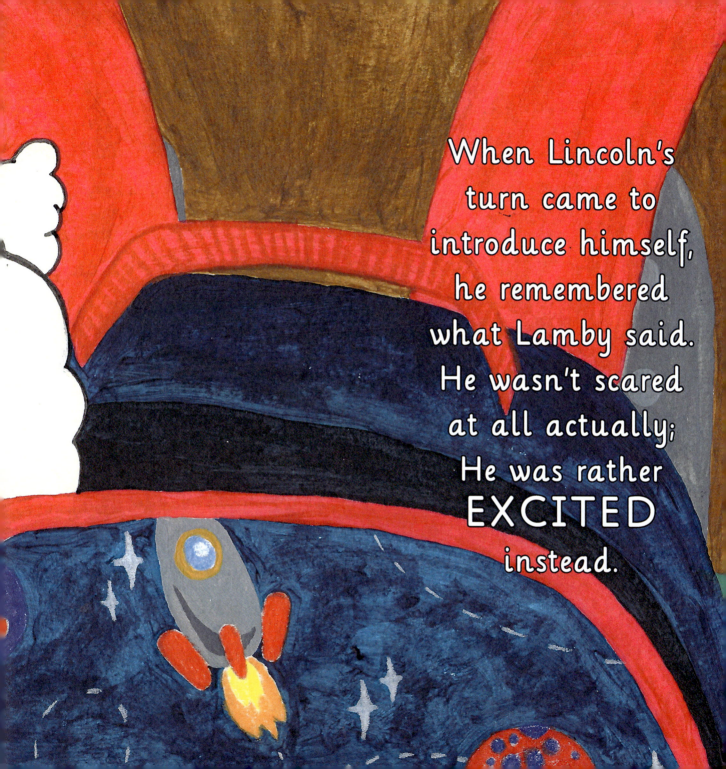

When Lincoln's turn came to introduce himself, he remembered what Lamby said. He wasn't scared at all actually; He was rather EXCITED instead.

As the day went on,
the fear was gone,
and a courageous
boy did appear.

Sometimes we need a
friend, indeed,
to help us to persevere.

The very next day, Lincoln got ready for school and decided to leave Lamby behind. She would be so proud of him for being brave, and he knew she wouldn't mind.

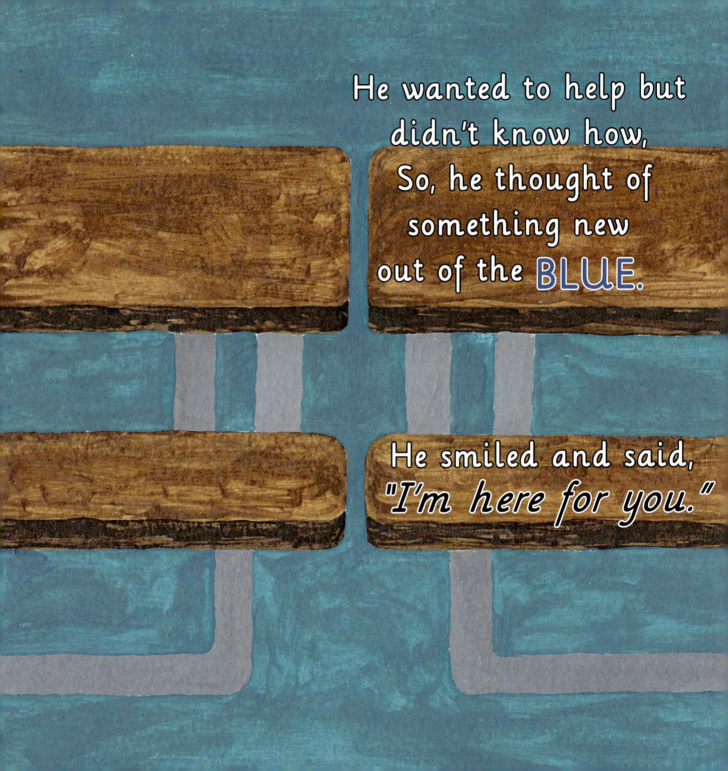

Just like his sweet little Lamby would do.

The rest of the day was full of laughter. There were no more tears from that point after.

Lincoln went home to tell Lamby of his day, She jumped for joy and shouted, "Yay, Hooray! See, I told you everything would be just fine, And that mommy would be back in no time."

He gave her a big hug and whispered in her ear "Thank you Lamby, for being here."

It's the spirit of Lamby that helps Lincoln at his best.

ABOUT THE AUTHOR

ROBYN MATOS

Writing has long been a passion of Robyn's, dating back to winning contests in elementary school, and having articles published in the local newspaper.

For her, there is just something so serene about fine-tuning a beautifully written soiree of words and bringing it to life. The thing about having a passion is to never give up on achieving them, no matter the difficulty, and no matter the age you begin. Expect to find more published material of Robyn's in the future! For now, enjoy the work inspired by her sweet son, Lincoln.

Made in United States
North Haven, CT
19 December 2022